Read and Rhyme LEVEL 3 ★★★

A Drink of Pink Ink

by Spencer Brinker

Consultant:
Beth Gambro
Reading Specialist
Yorkville, Illinois

Contents

BEARPORT PUBLISHING

New York, New York

A Drink of Pink Ink

Benjamin **Fink**
was trying
to **think**.

Where did
he put his jar
of **pink ink**?

Mr. **Fink** didn't see it near his pet **mink**.

Did he leave his **ink** at the ice-skating **rink**?

Benjamin was thirsty and reached for a **drink**.

That's when he smelled a terrible **stink**.

Inside his **drink** was the missing **pink ink**!

Key Words in the **-ink** Family

drink

ink

mink

pink

rink

sink

stink

think

Other **-ink** Words: **blink, brink, link, shrink**

Index

About the Author

Spencer Brinker loves to tell "dad jokes" and play word games with his twin girls.

Teaching Tips

Before Reading

✔ Introduce rhyming words and the **–ink** word family to readers.

✔ Guide readers on a "picture walk" through the text by asking them to name the things shown.

✔ Discuss book structure by showing children where text will appear consistently on pages. Highlight the supportive pattern of the book.

During Reading

✔ Encourage readers to "read with your finger" and point to each word as it is read. Stop periodically to ask children to point to a specific word in the text.

✔ Reading strategies: When encountering unknown words, prompt readers with encouraging cues such as:

- **Does that word look like a word you already know?**
- **Does it rhyme with another word you have already read?**

After Reading

✔ Write the key words on index cards.

- **Have readers match them to pictures in the book.**

✔ Ask readers to identify their favorite page in the book. Have them read that page aloud.

✔ Choose an **–ink** word. Ask children to pick a word that rhymes with it.

✔ Ask children to create their own rhymes using **–ink** words. Encourage them to use the same pattern found in the book.

Credits: Cover, © Tim UR/Shutterstock, © Prostock-studio/Shutterstock, and © timquo/Shutterstock; 2–3, © Cookie Studio/Shutterstock; 4–5, © Cookie Studio/Shutterstock and © timquo/Shutterstock; 6–7, © harmpeti/Shutterstock; 8–9, © Eric Isselee/Shutterstock and © Anurak Pongpatimet/Shutterstock; 10–11, © Cookie Studio/Shutterstock and © SeventyFour/Shutterstock; 12–13, © ArtBitz/Shutterstock and © Tim UR/Shutterstock; 14, © Cookie Studio/Shutterstock; 15, © Tim UR/Shutterstock, © Prostock-studio/Shutterstock, and © timquo/Shutterstock; 16T (L to R), © polya_olya/Shutterstock, © bogdan ionescu/Shutterstock, and © Eric Isselee/Shutterstock; 16B (L to R), © Cookie Studio/Shutterstock, © iiiphevgeniy/Shutterstock, © Eric Isselee/Shutterstock, and © Cookie Studio/Shutterstock.

Publisher: Kenn Goin   **Senior Editor:** Joyce Tavolacci   **Creative Director:** Spencer Brinker

Library of Congress Cataloging-in-Publication Data: Names: Brinker, Spencer, author. | Gambro, Beth, consultant. Title: A drink of pink ink / by Spencer Brinker; consultant: Beth Gambro, Reading Specialist, Yorkville, Illinois. Description: New York, New York: Bearport Publishing, [2020] | Series: Read and rhyme: Level 3 | Includes index. Identifiers: LCCN 2019007161 (print) | LCCN 2019012630 (ebook) | ISBN 9781642806144 (Ebook) | ISBN 9781642805604 (library) | ISBN 9781642807196 (pbk.) Subjects: LCSH: Readers (Primary) | Lost articles—Juvenile fiction. Classification: LCC PE1119 (ebook) | LCC PE1119 .B751834 2020 (print) | DDC 428.6/2—dc23 LC record available at https://lccn.loc.gov/2019007161

10 9 8 7 6 5 4 3 2 1